Color Library Animal Series

KITTENS

Designed and Produced by
Ted Smart & David Gibbon

COLOUR LIBRARY INTERNATIONAL

INTRODUCTION

If there is one creature we bring into our homes that never fails to captivate, it is a kitten. And yet, a new-born kitten is by no means a pretty thing. For many days it is a wriggling little creature, blind and apparently unaware of its surroundings, making soft sucking noises and smelling predominantly of milk. Yet, after ten to fourteen days, when its eyes are fully opened, misty-blue and weak in their newness, the infant cat, thanks to the solicitous concern of its mother, is immaculately clean and ready to make its first forays from its birthplace into a new and quite alien world. Kittens at this stage are still, of course, very dependent on their mother, who will show them, by example, how to wash themselves and how to play and hunt. If there is any danger to her kittens the mother cat will pick them up by the scruff of the neck and carry them to a safer place.

Kittens learn quickly and are by nature very inquisitive. They are also lively and mischievous and these qualities, together with their fluffy appearance, appealing expression and tumbling, clown-like antics make them irresistible. To see a kitten encounter, for the first time, such things as chair legs, human feet, balls of wool, cotton reels and so on is immediately enough to elicit, from humans, those expressions of delight reserved for all tiny, fluffy creatures that act comically.

Being so appealing has its drawbacks, however. It is all too common for sweet little kittens to be bought, perhaps as a present for a child, without the realization that the little bundle of fluff and mischief will eventually grow into a cat and that at all stages, from very young to mature adult, pet ownership carries certain responsibilities. Pets are not toys; they cannot be simply left in a cupboard when the novelty wears off. They are living creatures that require proper housing, feeding and care, and unless all the problems are thought out carefully, suffering and unhappiness can easily become the legacy of a well-meaning, though thoughtless, gift.

There can be few things sadder than the unwanted young, and before any decision is finally made regarding the acquisition of a kitten, all the possible problems should be fully discussed, always bearing in mind that what is being considered is <u>cat</u> ownership and that the kitten stage is purely a temporary one.

The next thing to consider will probably concern the breed of kitten. Obviously there is no way anyone can reasonably offer advice on this; all kittens, and cats, are attractive in their own way, and no one breed is really superior to any other. This must, therefore, be a purely personal decision, and this is where cat breeders can help. Buying from a breeder means that you will at least know that the kitten will become a fully-grown Persian, Siamese, tortoiseshell or what have you, whereas kittens obtained from other sources are very much an unknown quantity. Whichever is chosen, enjoy the pleasure of your kitten and care for it, and it will reward you by being an equally enjoyable companion when it becomes a cat.

Left: White Persian kitten

These pages: Cream longhair kittens.

Overleaf left: Marmalade longhair, cream longhair and bicolored longhair kittens.

Overleaf right: Bicolored shorthair and blue shorthair.

Above and left: Tabby shorthair.

Below: Marmalade shorthair.

Right: Cream shorthair and marmalade shorthair.

Left: Cream Persian kitten.

Above: Blue Persian kittens and cream Persian kitten.

Right: White longhair kittens.

Below: Chinchilla kitten.

Above: Cream longhairs.
Right: Tabby longhairs.
Below: White longhair.
Left: Tabby longhairs.
Overleaf: Tabby-and-white shorthairs.

This page: Blue-cream longhair mother with cream longhair and blue longhair kittens.

Right: Young cream longhair cat.

This page: Seal-point Siamese kittens.

Right: A selection of Siamese kittens with varying points.

Above left: White longhair.
Above: Tabby-and-white shorthair
Right: Marmalade-and-white shorthair.
Below: Cream shorthair.
Left: Bicolored shorthair.
Overleaf: Blue Persian and cream Persian kittens.

Left: White shorthair.
Above: Cream Persian.
Right: Tabby shorthair.
Below: Cream longhair.
Below left: Cream Persian and blue
Persian kittens.

Left and below: Tabby-and-white shorthair.
Above: Tabby shorthair kittens.
Right: Black-and-white shorthair.
Below left: Marmalade-and-white shorthair kittens.

Above: Blue longhair kittens.
Right: Blue-cream longhair cat wi[t]
blue longhair and cream longhair
kittens.
Below: Black longhair kitten.
Left: Tabby longhair kittens.